Daily Planner

DATE _______________   S M T W T F S

TOP 3 PRIORITIES

| 1. | 2. | 3. |

MORNING

TIME   TO DO   TIME   TO DO

AFTERNOON

TIME   TO DO   TIME   TO DO

EVENING

TIME   TO DO   TIME   TO DO

TODAY'S AFFIRMATIONS   *Notes*   **FOR TOMORROW**

Today, I will.

Daily Planner

DATE

S M T W T F S

TOP 3 PRIORITIES

1.

2.

3.

MORNING

TIME — TO DO

TIME — TO DO

AFTERNOON

TIME — TO DO

TIME — TO DO

EVENING

TIME — TO DO

TIME — TO DO

TODAY'S AFFIRMATIONS

Notes

FOR TOMORROW

Today, I will.

Daily Planner

DATE ___________________ S M T W T F S

TOP 3 PRIORITIES

1.

2.

3.

MORNING

TIME	TO DO		TIME	TO DO
◯			◯	
◯			◯	
◯			◯	

AFTERNOON

TIME	TO DO		TIME	TO DO
◯			◯	
◯			◯	
◯			◯	

EVENING

TIME	TO DO		TIME	TO DO
◯			◯	
◯			◯	
◯			◯	

TODAY'S AFFIRMATIONS

Notes

FOR TOMORROW

Today, I will.

Daily Planner

DATE ______________________ S M T W T F S

TOP 3 PRIORITIES

1. | 2. | 3.

MORNING

TIME TO DO TIME TO DO

AFTERNOON

TIME TO DO TIME TO DO

EVENING

TIME TO DO TIME TO DO

TODAY'S AFFIRMATIONS *Notes* FOR TOMORROW

Today, I will.

Daily Planner

DATE ___________________ S M T W T F S

TOP 3 PRIORITIES

1.

2.

3.

MORNING

TIME   TO DO   TIME   TO DO

AFTERNOON

TIME   TO DO   TIME   TO DO

EVENING

TIME   TO DO   TIME   TO DO

TODAY'S AFFIRMATIONS   *Notes*   **FOR TOMORROW**

Today, I will.

Daily Planner

S M T W T F S

TOP 3 PRIORITIES

1.

2.

3.

MORNING

TIME   TO DO

TIME   TO DO

AFTERNOON

TIME   TO DO

TIME   TO DO

EVENING

TIME   TO DO

TIME   TO DO

TODAY'S AFFIRMATIONS

Notes

FOR TOMORROW

Today, I will.

Daily Planner

DATE   S   M   T   W   T   F   S

TOP 3 PRIORITIES

1.

2.

3.

MORNING

TIME   TO DO   TIME   TO DO

AFTERNOON

TIME   TO DO   TIME   TO DO

EVENING

TIME   TO DO   TIME   TO DO

TODAY'S AFFIRMATIONS   *Notes*   FOR TOMORROW

Today, I will.

Daily Planner

DATE _______________ S M T W T F S

TOP 3 PRIORITIES

| 1. | 2. | 3. |

MORNING

TIME	TO DO		TIME	TO DO
○			○	
○			○	
○			○	

AFTERNOON

TIME	TO DO		TIME	TO DO
○			○	
○			○	
○			○	

EVENING

TIME	TO DO		TIME	TO DO
○			○	
○			○	
○			○	

TODAY'S AFFIRMATIONS   *Notes*   FOR TOMORROW

Today, I will.

Daily Planner

DATE ___________________   S M T W T F S

TOP 3 PRIORITIES

| 1. | 2. | 3. |

MORNING

TIME TO DO

○ ______ _______________________
○ ______ _______________________
○ ______ _______________________

TIME TO DO

○ ______ _______________________
○ ______ _______________________
○ ______ _______________________

AFTERNOON

TIME TO DO

○ ______ _______________________
○ ______ _______________________
○ ______ _______________________

TIME TO DO

○ ______ _______________________
○ ______ _______________________
○ ______ _______________________

EVENING

TIME TO DO

○ ______ _______________________
○ ______ _______________________
○ ______ _______________________

TIME TO DO

○ ______ _______________________
○ ______ _______________________
○ ______ _______________________

TODAY'S AFFIRMATIONS

Notes

FOR TOMORROW

Today, I will.

Daily Planner

DATE _______________   S M T W T F S

TOP 3 PRIORITIES

1. | 2. | 3.

MORNING

	TIME	TO DO			TIME	TO DO
○	______	____________		○	______	____________
○	______	____________		○	______	____________
○	______	____________		○	______	____________

AFTERNOON

	TIME	TO DO			TIME	TO DO
○	______	____________		○	______	____________
○	______	____________		○	______	____________
○	______	____________		○	______	____________

EVENING

	TIME	TO DO			TIME	TO DO
○	______	____________		○	______	____________
○	______	____________		○	______	____________
○	______	____________		○	______	____________

TODAY'S AFFIRMATIONS   Notes   FOR TOMORROW

Today, I will.

Daily Planner

DATE ____________________   S M T W T F S

TOP 3 PRIORITIES

1.	2.	3.

MORNING

TIME	TO DO		TIME	TO DO
○			○	
○			○	
○			○	

AFTERNOON

TIME	TO DO		TIME	TO DO
○			○	
○			○	
○			○	

EVENING

TIME	TO DO		TIME	TO DO
○			○	
○			○	
○			○	

TODAY'S AFFIRMATIONS   *Notes*   FOR TOMORROW

Today, I will.

Daily Planner

DATE _______________ S M T W T F S

TOP 3 PRIORITIES

1.

2.

3.

MORNING

TIME   TO DO   TIME   TO DO

AFTERNOON

TIME   TO DO   TIME   TO DO

EVENING

TIME   TO DO   TIME   TO DO

TODAY'S AFFIRMATIONS   *Notes*   **FOR TOMORROW**

Today, I will.

Daily Planner

DATE

S M T W T F S

TOP 3 PRIORITIES

1.

2.

3.

MORNING

TIME	TO DO

TIME	TO DO

AFTERNOON

TIME	TO DO

TIME	TO DO

EVENING

TIME	TO DO

TIME	TO DO

TODAY'S AFFIRMATIONS

Notes

FOR TOMORROW

Today, I will.

Daily Planner

DATE _______________ S M T W T F S

TOP 3 PRIORITIES

1.

2.

3.

MORNING

TIME   TO DO

TIME   TO DO

AFTERNOON

TIME   TO DO

TIME   TO DO

EVENING

TIME   TO DO

TIME   TO DO

TODAY'S AFFIRMATIONS

Notes

FOR TOMORROW

Today, I will.

Daily Planner

DATE ___________________________   S M T W T F S

TOP 3 PRIORITIES

1.

2.

3.

MORNING

TIME   TO DO   TIME   TO DO

AFTERNOON

TIME   TO DO   TIME   TO DO

EVENING

TIME   TO DO   TIME   TO DO

TODAY'S AFFIRMATIONS   *Notes*   **FOR TOMORROW**

Today, I will.

Daily Planner

DATE _______________ S M T W T F S

TOP 3 PRIORITIES

1.

2.

3.

MORNING

TIME TO DO

TIME TO DO

AFTERNOON

TIME TO DO

TIME TO DO

EVENING

TIME TO DO

TIME TO DO

TODAY'S AFFIRMATIONS

Notes

FOR TOMORROW

Today, I will.

Daily Planner

DATE ___________________   S M T W T F S

TOP 3 PRIORITIES

1.

2.

3.

MORNING

TIME   TO DO   TIME   TO DO

AFTERNOON

TIME   TO DO   TIME   TO DO

EVENING

TIME   TO DO   TIME   TO DO

TODAY'S AFFIRMATIONS   *Notes*   FOR TOMORROW

Today, I will.

Daily Planner

DATE _______________________   S M T W T F S

TOP 3 PRIORITIES

1.

2.

3.

MORNING

TIME	TO DO		TIME	TO DO
○			○	
○			○	
○			○	

AFTERNOON

TIME	TO DO		TIME	TO DO
○			○	
○			○	
○			○	

EVENING

TIME	TO DO		TIME	TO DO
○			○	
○			○	
○			○	

TODAY'S AFFIRMATIONS   *Notes*   ## FOR TOMORROW

Today, I will.

Daily Planner

DATE ___________________   S M T W T F S

TOP 3 PRIORITIES

1.

2.

3.

MORNING

TIME   TO DO   TIME   TO DO

AFTERNOON

TIME   TO DO   TIME   TO DO

EVENING

TIME   TO DO   TIME   TO DO

TODAY'S AFFIRMATIONS   *Notes*   FOR TOMORROW

Today, I will.

Daily Planner

DATE   S M T W T F S

TOP 3 PRIORITIES

1.

2.

3.

MORNING

TIME   TO DO   TIME   TO DO

AFTERNOON

TIME   TO DO   TIME   TO DO

EVENING

TIME   TO DO   TIME   TO DO

TODAY'S AFFIRMATIONS   Notes   FOR TOMORROW

Today, I will.

Daily Planner

DATE S M T W T F S

TOP 3 PRIORITIES

1.

2.

3.

MORNING

TIME	TO DO		TIME	TO DO
○			○	
○			○	
○			○	

AFTERNOON

TIME	TO DO		TIME	TO DO
○			○	
○			○	
○			○	

EVENING

TIME	TO DO		TIME	TO DO
○			○	
○			○	
○			○	

TODAY'S AFFIRMATIONS   *Notes*   FOR TOMORROW

Today, I will.

Daily Planner

DATE ____________________   S M T W T F S

TOP 3 PRIORITIES

1.

2.

3.

MORNING

TIME   TO DO

TIME   TO DO

AFTERNOON

TIME   TO DO

TIME   TO DO

EVENING

TIME   TO DO

TIME   TO DO

TODAY'S AFFIRMATIONS   *Notes*   FOR TOMORROW

Today, I will.

Daily Planner

DATE __________________   S M T W T F S

TOP 3 PRIORITIES

1.

2.

3.

MORNING

TIME   TO DO   TIME   TO DO

AFTERNOON

TIME   TO DO   TIME   TO DO

EVENING

TIME   TO DO   TIME   TO DO

TODAY'S AFFIRMATIONS   *Notes*   **FOR TOMORROW**

Today, I will.

Daily Planner

DATE _______________________ S M T W T F S

TOP 3 PRIORITIES

1.

2.

3.

MORNING

| TIME | TO DO | | TIME | TO DO |

AFTERNOON

| TIME | TO DO | | TIME | TO DO |

EVENING

| TIME | TO DO | | TIME | TO DO |

TODAY'S AFFIRMATIONS

Notes

FOR TOMORROW

Today, I will.

Daily Planner

DATE ___________________ S M T W T F S

TOP 3 PRIORITIES

1.

2.

3.

MORNING

TIME | TO DO   TIME | TO DO

AFTERNOON

TIME | TO DO   TIME | TO DO

EVENING

TIME | TO DO   TIME | TO DO

TODAY'S AFFIRMATIONS   *Notes*   **FOR TOMORROW**

Today, I will.

Daily Planner

DATE ___________________________   S M T W T F S

TOP 3 PRIORITIES

1.

2.

3.

MORNING

| TIME | TO DO | | TIME | TO DO |

AFTERNOON

| TIME | TO DO | | TIME | TO DO |

EVENING

| TIME | TO DO | | TIME | TO DO |

TODAY'S AFFIRMATIONS

Notes

FOR TOMORROW

Today, I will.

Daily Planner

DATE _______________   S M T W T F S

TOP 3 PRIORITIES

1.

2.

3.

MORNING

TIME   TO DO   TIME   TO DO

AFTERNOON

TIME   TO DO   TIME   TO DO

EVENING

TIME   TO DO   TIME   TO DO

TODAY'S AFFIRMATIONS   *Notes*   FOR TOMORROW

Today, I will.

Daily Planner

DATE ______________________   S M T W T F S

TOP 3 PRIORITIES

1.

2.

3.

MORNING

TIME   TO DO   TIME   TO DO

AFTERNOON

TIME   TO DO   TIME   TO DO

EVENING

TIME   TO DO   TIME   TO DO

TODAY'S AFFIRMATIONS   *Notes*   **FOR TOMORROW**

Today, I will.

Daily Planner

DATE ___________________   S M T W T F S

TOP 3 PRIORITIES

1.

2.

3.

MORNING

| TIME | TO DO | | TIME | TO DO |

AFTERNOON

| TIME | TO DO | | TIME | TO DO |

EVENING

| TIME | TO DO | | TIME | TO DO |

TODAY'S AFFIRMATIONS   *Notes*   **FOR TOMORROW**

Today, I will.

Daily Planner

DATE ____________________   S M T W T F S

TOP 3 PRIORITIES

1.

2.

3.

MORNING

TIME   TO DO   TIME   TO DO

AFTERNOON

TIME   TO DO   TIME   TO DO

EVENING

TIME   TO DO   TIME   TO DO

TODAY'S AFFIRMATIONS   *Notes*   FOR TOMORROW

Today, I will.

Daily Planner

TOP 3 PRIORITIES

1.

2.

3.

MORNING

TIME	TO DO		TIME	TO DO

AFTERNOON

TIME	TO DO		TIME	TO DO

EVENING

TIME	TO DO		TIME	TO DO

TODAY'S AFFIRMATIONS *Notes* **FOR TOMORROW**

Today, I will.

Daily Planner

DATE ___________________ S M T W T F S

TOP 3 PRIORITIES

1.

2.

3.

MORNING

TIME TO DO   TIME TO DO

AFTERNOON

TIME TO DO   TIME TO DO

EVENING

TIME TO DO   TIME TO DO

TODAY'S AFFIRMATIONS   *Notes*   **FOR TOMORROW**

Today, I will.

Daily Planner

S M T W T F S

TOP 3 PRIORITIES

1.

2.

3.

MORNING

TIME | TO DO

TIME | TO DO

AFTERNOON

TIME | TO DO

TIME | TO DO

EVENING

TIME | TO DO

TIME | TO DO

TODAY'S AFFIRMATIONS

Notes

FOR TOMORROW

Today, I will.

Daily Planner

DATE ____________________   S M T W T F S

TOP 3 PRIORITIES

1.

2.

3.

MORNING

TIME   TO DO   TIME   TO DO

AFTERNOON

TIME   TO DO   TIME   TO DO

EVENING

TIME   TO DO   TIME   TO DO

TODAY'S AFFIRMATIONS   *Notes*   FOR TOMORROW

Today, I will.

Daily Planner

DATE ______________________   S M T W T F S

TOP 3 PRIORITIES

1.

2.

3.

MORNING

| TIME | TO DO | | TIME | TO DO |

AFTERNOON

| TIME | TO DO | | TIME | TO DO |

EVENING

| TIME | TO DO | | TIME | TO DO |

TODAY'S AFFIRMATIONS

Notes

FOR TOMORROW

Today, I will.

Daily Planner

DATE ________________________ S M T W T F S

TOP 3 PRIORITIES

1.

2.

3.

MORNING

TIME   TO DO   TIME   TO DO

AFTERNOON

TIME   TO DO   TIME   TO DO

EVENING

TIME   TO DO   TIME   TO DO

TODAY'S AFFIRMATIONS   *Notes*   FOR TOMORROW

Today, I will.

Daily Planner

DATE _______________________ S M T W T F S

TOP 3 PRIORITIES

1.

2.

3.

MORNING

TIME TO DO

TIME TO DO

AFTERNOON

TIME TO DO

TIME TO DO

EVENING

TIME TO DO

TIME TO DO

TODAY'S AFFIRMATIONS *Notes* **FOR TOMORROW**

Today, I will.

Daily Planner

TOP 3 PRIORITIES

1.

2.

3.

MORNING

| TIME | TO DO | | TIME | TO DO |

AFTERNOON

| TIME | TO DO | | TIME | TO DO |

EVENING

| TIME | TO DO | | TIME | TO DO |

TODAY'S AFFIRMATIONS

Notes

FOR TOMORROW

Today, I will.

Daily Planner

DATE ______________________ S M T W T F S

TOP 3 PRIORITIES

1.
2.
3.

MORNING

TIME   TO DO   TIME   TO DO

AFTERNOON

TIME   TO DO   TIME   TO DO

EVENING

TIME   TO DO   TIME   TO DO

TODAY'S AFFIRMATIONS   *Notes*   **FOR TOMORROW**

Today, I will.

Daily Planner

S M T W T F S

TOP 3 PRIORITIES

1.

2.

3.

MORNING

TIME — TO DO

TIME — TO DO

AFTERNOON

TIME — TO DO

TIME — TO DO

EVENING

TIME — TO DO

TIME — TO DO

TODAY'S AFFIRMATIONS

Notes

FOR TOMORROW

Today, I will.

Daily Planner

DATE

S M T W T F S

TOP 3 PRIORITIES

1.

2.

3.

MORNING

TIME   TO DO   TIME   TO DO

AFTERNOON

TIME   TO DO   TIME   TO DO

EVENING

TIME   TO DO   TIME   TO DO

TODAY'S AFFIRMATIONS

Notes

FOR TOMORROW

Today, I will.

Daily Planner

DATE ______________ S M T W T F S

TOP 3 PRIORITIES

1.

2.

3.

MORNING

TIME   TO DO   TIME   TO DO

AFTERNOON

TIME   TO DO   TIME   TO DO

EVENING

TIME   TO DO   TIME   TO DO

TODAY'S AFFIRMATIONS   *Notes*   **FOR TOMORROW**

Today, I will.

Daily Planner

DATE ___________________   S M T W T F S

TOP 3 PRIORITIES

1.

2.

3.

MORNING

TIME	TO DO
○ ______	______________
○ ______	______________
○ ______	______________

TIME	TO DO
○ ______	______________
○ ______	______________
○ ______	______________

AFTERNOON

TIME	TO DO
○ ______	______________
○ ______	______________
○ ______	______________

TIME	TO DO
○ ______	______________
○ ______	______________
○ ______	______________

EVENING

TIME	TO DO
○ ______	______________
○ ______	______________
○ ______	______________

TIME	TO DO
○ ______	______________
○ ______	______________
○ ______	______________

TODAY'S AFFIRMATIONS

Notes

FOR TOMORROW

Today, I will.

Daily Planner

DATE __________________   S M T W T F S

TOP 3 PRIORITIES

1.

2.

3.

MORNING

TIME   TO DO   TIME   TO DO

AFTERNOON

TIME   TO DO   TIME   TO DO

EVENING

TIME   TO DO   TIME   TO DO

TODAY'S AFFIRMATIONS   *Notes*   **FOR TOMORROW**

Today, I will.

Daily Planner

DATE ________________ S M T W T F S

TOP 3 PRIORITIES

1.

2.

3.

MORNING

TIME · TO DO   TIME · TO DO

AFTERNOON

TIME · TO DO   TIME · TO DO

EVENING

TIME · TO DO   TIME · TO DO

TODAY'S AFFIRMATIONS · *Notes* · **FOR TOMORROW**

Today, I will.

Daily Planner

DATE ___________________   S M T W T F S

TOP 3 PRIORITIES

1.

2.

3.

MORNING

TIME   TO DO   TIME   TO DO

AFTERNOON

TIME   TO DO   TIME   TO DO

EVENING

TIME   TO DO   TIME   TO DO

TODAY'S AFFIRMATIONS   *Notes*   **FOR TOMORROW**

Today, I will.

Daily Planner

DATE _______________________   S M T W T F S

TOP 3 PRIORITIES

1.

2.

3.

MORNING

TIME	TO DO		TIME	TO DO
○			○	
○			○	
○			○	

AFTERNOON

TIME	TO DO		TIME	TO DO
○			○	
○			○	
○			○	

EVENING

TIME	TO DO		TIME	TO DO
○			○	
○			○	
○			○	

TODAY'S AFFIRMATIONS   *Notes*   **FOR TOMORROW**

Today, I will.

Daily Planner

DATE _______________ S M T W T F S

TOP 3 PRIORITIES

1.

2.

3.

MORNING

TIME TO DO

TIME TO DO

AFTERNOON

TIME TO DO

TIME TO DO

EVENING

TIME TO DO

TIME TO DO

TODAY'S AFFIRMATIONS

Notes

FOR TOMORROW

Today, I will.

Daily Planner

DATE ___________________ S M T W T F S

TOP 3 PRIORITIES

1.

2.

3.

MORNING

TIME | TO DO | TIME | TO DO

AFTERNOON

TIME | TO DO | TIME | TO DO

EVENING

TIME | TO DO | TIME | TO DO

TODAY'S AFFIRMATIONS

Notes

FOR TOMORROW

Today, I will.

Daily Planner

DATE ________________________ S M T W T F S

TOP 3 PRIORITIES

1.

2.

3.

MORNING

TIME   TO DO   TIME   TO DO

AFTERNOON

TIME   TO DO   TIME   TO DO

EVENING

TIME   TO DO   TIME   TO DO

TODAY'S AFFIRMATIONS   *Notes*   FOR TOMORROW

Today, I will.

Daily Planner

DATE ______________________   S M T W T F S

TOP 3 PRIORITIES

1.

2.

3.

MORNING

TIME   TO DO   TIME   TO DO

AFTERNOON

TIME   TO DO   TIME   TO DO

EVENING

TIME   TO DO   TIME   TO DO

TODAY'S AFFIRMATIONS   *Notes*   **FOR TOMORROW**

Today, I will.

Daily Planner

DATE ___________________ S M T W T F S

TOP 3 PRIORITIES

1.

2.

3.

MORNING

TIME TO DO TIME TO DO

AFTERNOON

TIME TO DO TIME TO DO

EVENING

TIME TO DO TIME TO DO

TODAY'S AFFIRMATIONS *Notes* FOR TOMORROW

Today, I will.

Daily Planner

DATE ______________________   S M T W T F S

TOP 3 PRIORITIES

1.

2.

3.

MORNING

TIME   TO DO   TIME   TO DO

AFTERNOON

TIME   TO DO   TIME   TO DO

EVENING

TIME   TO DO   TIME   TO DO

TODAY'S AFFIRMATIONS   *Notes*   **FOR TOMORROW**

Today, I will.

Daily Planner

DATE ___________________

S M T W T F S

TOP 3 PRIORITIES

1.

2.

3.

MORNING

TIME   TO DO   TIME   TO DO

AFTERNOON

TIME   TO DO   TIME   TO DO

EVENING

TIME   TO DO   TIME   TO DO

TODAY'S AFFIRMATIONS

Notes

FOR TOMORROW

Today, I will.

Daily Planner

DATE ___________________ S M T W T F S

TOP 3 PRIORITIES

1.

2.

3.

MORNING

TIME TO DO

TIME TO DO

AFTERNOON

TIME TO DO

TIME TO DO

EVENING

TIME TO DO

TIME TO DO

TODAY'S AFFIRMATIONS *Notes* FOR TOMORROW

Today, I will.

Daily Planner

DATE _______________   S M T W T F S

TOP 3 PRIORITIES

1.

2.

3.

MORNING

TIME   TO DO   TIME   TO DO

AFTERNOON

TIME   TO DO   TIME   TO DO

EVENING

TIME   TO DO   TIME   TO DO

TODAY'S AFFIRMATIONS   *Notes*   **FOR TOMORROW**

Today, I will.

Daily Planner

DATE   S M T W T F S

TOP 3 PRIORITIES

1.

2.

3.

MORNING

| TIME | TO DO | TIME | TO DO |

AFTERNOON

| TIME | TO DO | TIME | TO DO |

EVENING

| TIME | TO DO | TIME | TO DO |

TODAY'S AFFIRMATIONS   *Notes*   **FOR TOMORROW**

Today, I will.

Daily Planner

DATE ______________________   S M T W T F S

TOP 3 PRIORITIES

1.

2.

3.

MORNING

TIME TO DO   TIME TO DO

AFTERNOON

TIME TO DO   TIME TO DO

EVENING

TIME TO DO   TIME TO DO

TODAY'S AFFIRMATIONS   *Notes*   **FOR TOMORROW**

Today, I will.

Daily Planner

DATE

S M T W T F S

TOP 3 PRIORITIES

1.

2.

3.

MORNING

TIME   TO DO   TIME   TO DO

AFTERNOON

TIME   TO DO   TIME   TO DO

EVENING

TIME   TO DO   TIME   TO DO

TODAY'S AFFIRMATIONS   *Notes*   **FOR TOMORROW**

Today, I will.

Daily Planner

DATE ____________________   S M T W T F S

TOP 3 PRIORITIES

1.

2.

3.

MORNING

TIME   TO DO   TIME   TO DO

AFTERNOON

TIME   TO DO   TIME   TO DO

EVENING

TIME   TO DO   TIME   TO DO

TODAY'S AFFIRMATIONS   *Notes*   **FOR TOMORROW**

Today, I will.

Daily Planner

DATE ________________________   S M T W T F S

TOP 3 PRIORITIES

1.

2.

3.

MORNING

TIME	TO DO

TIME	TO DO

AFTERNOON

TIME	TO DO

TIME	TO DO

EVENING

TIME	TO DO

TIME	TO DO

TODAY'S AFFIRMATIONS   *Notes*   **FOR TOMORROW**

Today I will.

Daily Planner

DATE ____________________   S   M   T   W   T   F   S

TOP 3 PRIORITIES

1.

2.

3.

MORNING

TIME   TO DO   TIME   TO DO

AFTERNOON

TIME   TO DO   TIME   TO DO

EVENING

TIME   TO DO   TIME   TO DO

TODAY'S AFFIRMATIONS   *Notes*   **FOR TOMORROW**

Today, I will.

Daily Planner

DATE ______________________   S M T W T F S

TOP 3 PRIORITIES

1.

2.

3.

MORNING

TIME	TO DO		TIME	TO DO
○ ____	__________		○ ____	__________
○ ____	__________		○ ____	__________
○ ____	__________		○ ____	__________

AFTERNOON

TIME	TO DO		TIME	TO DO
○ ____	__________		○ ____	__________
○ ____	__________		○ ____	__________
○ ____	__________		○ ____	__________

EVENING

TIME	TO DO		TIME	TO DO
○ ____	__________		○ ____	__________
○ ____	__________		○ ____	__________
○ ____	__________		○ ____	__________

TODAY'S AFFIRMATIONS   *Notes*   FOR TOMORROW

Today, I will.

Daily Planner

DATE _______________ S M T W T F S

TOP 3 PRIORITIES

1.

2.

3.

MORNING

TIME TO DO   TIME TO DO

AFTERNOON

TIME TO DO   TIME TO DO

EVENING

TIME TO DO   TIME TO DO

TODAY'S AFFIRMATIONS   *Notes*   FOR TOMORROW

Today, I will.

Daily Planner

DATE _______________ S M T W T F S

TOP 3 PRIORITIES

1.	2.	3.

MORNING

TIME   TO DO   TIME   TO DO

○ _______ ___________________ ○ _______ ___________________
○ _______ ___________________ ○ _______ ___________________
○ _______ ___________________ ○ _______ ___________________

AFTERNOON

TIME   TO DO   TIME   TO DO

○ _______ ___________________ ○ _______ ___________________
○ _______ ___________________ ○ _______ ___________________
○ _______ ___________________ ○ _______ ___________________

EVENING

TIME   TO DO   TIME   TO DO

○ _______ ___________________ ○ _______ ___________________
○ _______ ___________________ ○ _______ ___________________
○ _______ ___________________ ○ _______ ___________________

TODAY'S AFFIRMATIONS   *Notes*   FOR TOMORROW

Today, I will.

Daily Planner

TOP 3 PRIORITIES

1.

2.

3.

MORNING

TIME	TO DO		TIME	TO DO

AFTERNOON

TIME	TO DO		TIME	TO DO

EVENING

TIME	TO DO		TIME	TO DO

TODAY'S AFFIRMATIONS

Notes

FOR TOMORROW

Today, I will.

Daily Planner

DATE ___________________________   S M T W T F S

TOP 3 PRIORITIES

1.   2.   3.

MORNING

TIME   TO DO   TIME   TO DO

○ ______ __________   ○ ______ __________
○ ______ __________   ○ ______ __________
○ ______ __________   ○ ______ __________

AFTERNOON

TIME   TO DO   TIME   TO DO

○ ______ __________   ○ ______ __________
○ ______ __________   ○ ______ __________
○ ______ __________   ○ ______ __________

EVENING

TIME   TO DO   TIME   TO DO

○ ______ __________   ○ ______ __________
○ ______ __________   ○ ______ __________
○ ______ __________   ○ ______ __________

TODAY'S AFFIRMATIONS   *Notes*   FOR TOMORROW

Today, I will.

Daily Planner

DATE ______________________   S M T W T F S

TOP 3 PRIORITIES

1.

2.

3.

MORNING

TIME   TO DO   TIME   TO DO

AFTERNOON

TIME   TO DO   TIME   TO DO

EVENING

TIME   TO DO   TIME   TO DO

TODAY'S AFFIRMATIONS   *Notes*   **FOR TOMORROW**

Today, I will.

Daily Planner

DATE

S M T W T F S

TOP 3 PRIORITIES

1.

2.

3.

MORNING

TIME   TO DO

TIME   TO DO

AFTERNOON

TIME   TO DO

TIME   TO DO

EVENING

TIME   TO DO

TIME   TO DO

TODAY'S AFFIRMATIONS

Notes

FOR TOMORROW

Today, I will.

Daily Planner

DATE _______________ S M T W T F S

TOP 3 PRIORITIES

1.

2.

3.

MORNING

TIME   TO DO   TIME   TO DO

AFTERNOON

TIME   TO DO   TIME   TO DO

EVENING

TIME   TO DO   TIME   TO DO

TODAY'S AFFIRMATIONS   *Notes*   FOR TOMORROW

Today, I will.

Daily Planner

DATE ____________________   S M T W T F S

TOP 3 PRIORITIES

1.	2.	3.

MORNING

TIME	TO DO		TIME	TO DO
○			○	
○			○	
○			○	

AFTERNOON

TIME	TO DO		TIME	TO DO
○			○	
○			○	
○			○	

EVENING

TIME	TO DO		TIME	TO DO
○			○	
○			○	
○			○	

TODAY'S AFFIRMATIONS   *Notes*   **FOR TOMORROW**

Today, I will.

Daily Planner

DATE ________________________   S M T W T F S

TOP 3 PRIORITIES

1.

2.

3.

MORNING

TIME   TO DO   TIME   TO DO

AFTERNOON

TIME   TO DO   TIME   TO DO

EVENING

TIME   TO DO   TIME   TO DO

TODAY'S AFFIRMATIONS   *Notes*   **FOR TOMORROW**

Today, I will.

Daily Planner

DATE ______________________ S M T W T F S

TOP 3 PRIORITIES

1.

2.

3.

MORNING

| TIME | TO DO | | TIME | TO DO |

AFTERNOON

| TIME | TO DO | | TIME | TO DO |

EVENING

| TIME | TO DO | | TIME | TO DO |

TODAY'S AFFIRMATIONS   *Notes*   FOR TOMORROW

Today, I will.

Daily Planner

DATE _______________________   S M T W T F S

TOP 3 PRIORITIES

1.

2.

3.

MORNING

TIME	TO DO		TIME	TO DO

AFTERNOON

TIME	TO DO		TIME	TO DO

EVENING

TIME	TO DO		TIME	TO DO

TODAY'S AFFIRMATIONS

Notes

FOR TOMORROW

Today, I will.

Daily Planner

DATE   S M T W T F S

TOP 3 PRIORITIES

1.

2.

3.

MORNING

TIME   TO DO   TIME   TO DO

AFTERNOON

TIME   TO DO   TIME   TO DO

EVENING

TIME   TO DO   TIME   TO DO

TODAY'S AFFIRMATIONS   *Notes*   **FOR TOMORROW**

Today, I will.

Daily Planner

DATE _______________ S M T W T F S

TOP 3 PRIORITIES

1.
2.
3.

MORNING

TIME   TO DO   TIME   TO DO

AFTERNOON

TIME   TO DO   TIME   TO DO

EVENING

TIME   TO DO   TIME   TO DO

TODAY'S AFFIRMATIONS   *Notes*   FOR TOMORROW

Today, I will.

Daily Planner

DATE _______________________   S M T W T F S

TOP 3 PRIORITIES

1.

2.

3.

MORNING

TIME	TO DO		TIME	TO DO
○			○	
○			○	
○			○	

AFTERNOON

TIME	TO DO		TIME	TO DO
○			○	
○			○	
○			○	

EVENING

TIME	TO DO		TIME	TO DO
○			○	
○			○	
○			○	

TODAY'S AFFIRMATIONS   *Notes*   **FOR TOMORROW**

Today, I will.

Daily Planner

S M T W T F S

TOP 3 PRIORITIES

1.

2.

3.

MORNING

TIME   TO DO

TIME   TO DO

AFTERNOON

TIME   TO DO

TIME   TO DO

EVENING

TIME   TO DO

TIME   TO DO

TODAY'S AFFIRMATIONS

Notes

FOR TOMORROW

Today, I will.

Daily Planner

DATE _______________________   S M T W T F S

TOP 3 PRIORITIES

1.

2.

3.

MORNING

TIME   TO DO   TIME   TO DO

AFTERNOON

TIME   TO DO   TIME   TO DO

EVENING

TIME   TO DO   TIME   TO DO

TODAY'S AFFIRMATIONS   *Notes*   **FOR TOMORROW**

Today, I will.

Daily Planner

DATE ______________________   S   M   T   W   T   F   S

TOP 3 PRIORITIES

| 1. | 2. | 3. |

MORNING

TIME   TO DO   TIME   TO DO

AFTERNOON

TIME   TO DO   TIME   TO DO

EVENING

TIME   TO DO   TIME   TO DO

TODAY'S AFFIRMATIONS   *Notes*   ## FOR TOMORROW

Today, I will.

Daily Planner

DATE ______________________   S   M   T   W   T   F   S

TOP 3 PRIORITIES

1.

2.

3.

MORNING

TIME   TO DO   TIME   TO DO

AFTERNOON

TIME   TO DO   TIME   TO DO

EVENING

TIME   TO DO   TIME   TO DO

TODAY'S AFFIRMATIONS   *Notes*   FOR TOMORROW

Today, I will.

Daily Planner

DATE _______________ S M T W T F S

TOP 3 PRIORITIES

1.

2.

3.

MORNING

TIME TO DO

TIME TO DO

AFTERNOON

TIME TO DO

TIME TO DO

EVENING

TIME TO DO

TIME TO DO

TODAY'S AFFIRMATIONS

Notes

FOR TOMORROW

Today, I will.

Daily Planner

DATE ____________________   S M T W T F S

TOP 3 PRIORITIES

1.

2.

3.

MORNING

TIME   TO DO   TIME   TO DO

AFTERNOON

TIME   TO DO   TIME   TO DO

EVENING

TIME   TO DO   TIME   TO DO

TODAY'S AFFIRMATIONS   *Notes*   **FOR TOMORROW**

Today, I will.

Daily Planner

DATE _______________   S M T W T F S

TOP 3 PRIORITIES

| 1. | 2. | 3. |

MORNING

TIME   TO DO   TIME   TO DO

AFTERNOON

TIME   TO DO   TIME   TO DO

EVENING

TIME   TO DO   TIME   TO DO

TODAY'S AFFIRMATIONS   *Notes*   **FOR TOMORROW**

Today, I will.

Daily Planner

DATE _______________ S M T W T F S

TOP 3 PRIORITIES

1.	2.	3.

MORNING

TIME	TO DO		TIME	TO DO
○			○	
○			○	
○			○	

AFTERNOON

TIME	TO DO		TIME	TO DO
○			○	
○			○	
○			○	

EVENING

TIME	TO DO		TIME	TO DO
○			○	
○			○	
○			○	

TODAY'S AFFIRMATIONS

Notes

FOR TOMORROW

Today, I will.

Daily Planner

DATE ___________________________ S M T W T F S

TOP 3 PRIORITIES

1.

2.

3.

MORNING

TIME   TO DO

TIME   TO DO

AFTERNOON

TIME   TO DO

TIME   TO DO

EVENING

TIME   TO DO

TIME   TO DO

TODAY'S AFFIRMATIONS

Notes

FOR TOMORROW

Today, I will.

Daily Planner

DATE ___________________   S M T W T F S

TOP 3 PRIORITIES

1.

2.

3.

MORNING

TIME	TO DO		TIME	TO DO

AFTERNOON

TIME	TO DO		TIME	TO DO

EVENING

TIME	TO DO		TIME	TO DO

TODAY'S AFFIRMATIONS   *Notes*   FOR TOMORROW

Today, I will.

Daily Planner

DATE _______________________ S M T W T F S

TOP 3 PRIORITIES

1.

2.

3.

MORNING

TIME TO DO

TIME TO DO

AFTERNOON

TIME TO DO

TIME TO DO

EVENING

TIME TO DO

TIME TO DO

TODAY'S AFFIRMATIONS

Notes

FOR TOMORROW

Today, I will.

Daily Planner

DATE ______________________ S M T W T F S

TOP 3 PRIORITIES

1.

2.

3.

MORNING

TIME   TO DO   TIME   TO DO

AFTERNOON

TIME   TO DO   TIME   TO DO

EVENING

TIME   TO DO   TIME   TO DO

TODAY'S AFFIRMATIONS   *Notes*   FOR TOMORROW

Today, I will.

Daily Planner

DATE _______________________ S M T W T F S

TOP 3 PRIORITIES

1.

2.

3.

MORNING

TIME   TO DO

TIME   TO DO

AFTERNOON

TIME   TO DO

TIME   TO DO

EVENING

TIME   TO DO

TIME   TO DO

TODAY'S AFFIRMATIONS

Notes

FOR TOMORROW

Today, I will.

Daily Planner

DATE ________________ S M T W T F S

TOP 3 PRIORITIES

1.

2.

3.

MORNING

TIME   TO DO   TIME   TO DO

AFTERNOON

TIME   TO DO   TIME   TO DO

EVENING

TIME   TO DO   TIME   TO DO

TODAY'S AFFIRMATIONS   *Notes*   **FOR TOMORROW**

Today, I will.

Daily Planner

TOP 3 PRIORITIES

1.

2.

3.

MORNING

TIME TO DO

TIME TO DO

AFTERNOON

TIME TO DO

TIME TO DO

EVENING

TIME TO DO

TIME TO DO

TODAY'S AFFIRMATIONS

Notes

FOR TOMORROW

Today, I will.

Daily Planner

TOP 3 PRIORITIES

1.

2.

3.

MORNING

TIME   TO DO   TIME   TO DO

AFTERNOON

TIME   TO DO   TIME   TO DO

EVENING

TIME   TO DO   TIME   TO DO

TODAY'S AFFIRMATIONS   *Notes*   FOR TOMORROW

Today, I will.

Daily Planner

DATE ____________________ S M T W T F S

TOP 3 PRIORITIES

1.

2.

3.

MORNING

TIME TO DO

TIME TO DO

AFTERNOON

TIME TO DO

TIME TO DO

EVENING

TIME TO DO

TIME TO DO

TODAY'S AFFIRMATIONS

Notes

FOR TOMORROW

Today, I will.

Daily Planner

DATE _______________________ S M T W T F S

TOP 3 PRIORITIES

1.

2.

3.

MORNING

TIME   TO DO   TIME   TO DO

AFTERNOON

TIME   TO DO   TIME   TO DO

EVENING

TIME   TO DO   TIME   TO DO

TODAY'S AFFIRMATIONS   *Notes*   FOR TOMORROW

Today, I will.

Daily Planner

DATE ______________________   S M T W T F S

TOP 3 PRIORITIES

1.

2.

3.

MORNING

TIME   TO DO   TIME   TO DO

AFTERNOON

TIME   TO DO   TIME   TO DO

EVENING

TIME   TO DO   TIME   TO DO

TODAY'S AFFIRMATIONS   *Notes*   **FOR TOMORROW**

Today, I will.

Daily Planner

DATE ______________________   S M T W T F S

TOP 3 PRIORITIES

1.

2.

3.

MORNING

| TIME | TO DO | | TIME | TO DO |

AFTERNOON

| TIME | TO DO | | TIME | TO DO |

EVENING

| TIME | TO DO | | TIME | TO DO |

TODAY'S AFFIRMATIONS   *Notes*   **FOR TOMORROW**

Today, I will.

Daily Planner

DATE _______________ S M T W T F S

TOP 3 PRIORITIES

1.

2.

3.

MORNING

TIME	TO DO		TIME	TO DO
○			○	
○			○	
○			○	

AFTERNOON

TIME	TO DO		TIME	TO DO
○			○	
○			○	
○			○	

EVENING

TIME	TO DO		TIME	TO DO
○			○	
○			○	
○			○	

TODAY'S AFFIRMATIONS   *Notes*   FOR TOMORROW

Today, I will.

Daily Planner

DATE ___________________   S M T W T F S

TOP 3 PRIORITIES

1.

2.

3.

MORNING

TIME   TO DO   TIME   TO DO

AFTERNOON

TIME   TO DO   TIME   TO DO

EVENING

TIME   TO DO   TIME   TO DO

TODAY'S AFFIRMATIONS   *Notes*   ## FOR TOMORROW

Today, I will.

Daily Planner

DATE ___________ S M T W T F S

TOP 3 PRIORITIES

1.

2.

3.

MORNING

TIME TO DO

TIME TO DO

AFTERNOON

TIME TO DO

TIME TO DO

EVENING

TIME TO DO

TIME TO DO

TODAY'S AFFIRMATIONS

Notes

FOR TOMORROW

Today, I will.

Daily Planner

DATE _______________________   S M T W T F S

TOP 3 PRIORITIES

1.

2.

3.

MORNING

| TIME | TO DO | | TIME | TO DO |

AFTERNOON

| TIME | TO DO | | TIME | TO DO |

EVENING

| TIME | TO DO | | TIME | TO DO |

TODAY'S AFFIRMATIONS   *Notes*   **FOR TOMORROW**

Today, I will.

Daily Planner

DATE   S M T W T F S

TOP 3 PRIORITIES

1.

2.

3.

MORNING

TIME   TO DO   TIME   TO DO

AFTERNOON

TIME   TO DO   TIME   TO DO

EVENING

TIME   TO DO   TIME   TO DO

TODAY'S AFFIRMATIONS   *Notes*   FOR TOMORROW

Today, I will.

Daily Planner

DATE   S M T W T F S

TOP 3 PRIORITIES

1.

2.

3.

MORNING

TIME	TO DO		TIME	TO DO

AFTERNOON

TIME	TO DO		TIME	TO DO

EVENING

TIME	TO DO		TIME	TO DO

TODAY'S AFFIRMATIONS   *Notes*   **FOR TOMORROW**

Today, I will.

Daily Planner

DATE ______________ S M T W T F S

TOP 3 PRIORITIES

1.

2.

3.

MORNING

TIME   TO DO   TIME   TO DO

AFTERNOON

TIME   TO DO   TIME   TO DO

EVENING

TIME   TO DO   TIME   TO DO

TODAY'S AFFIRMATIONS   *Notes*   FOR TOMORROW

Today, I will.

Daily Planner

DATE ______________________ S M T W T F S

TOP 3 PRIORITIES

1.

2.

3.

MORNING

TIME   TO DO   TIME   TO DO

AFTERNOON

TIME   TO DO   TIME   TO DO

EVENING

TIME   TO DO   TIME   TO DO

TODAY'S AFFIRMATIONS   *Notes*   **FOR TOMORROW**

Today, I will.

Daily Planner

DATE _______________ S M T W T F S

TOP 3 PRIORITIES

1.

2.

3.

MORNING

TIME   TO DO   TIME   TO DO

AFTERNOON

TIME   TO DO   TIME   TO DO

EVENING

TIME   TO DO   TIME   TO DO

TODAY'S AFFIRMATIONS   *Notes*   ## FOR TOMORROW

Today, I will.

Daily Planner

DATE ________________ S M T W T F S

TOP 3 PRIORITIES

1.

2.

3.

MORNING

TIME	TO DO		TIME	TO DO
○			○	
○			○	
○			○	

AFTERNOON

TIME	TO DO		TIME	TO DO
○			○	
○			○	
○			○	

EVENING

TIME	TO DO		TIME	TO DO
○			○	
○			○	
○			○	

TODAY'S AFFIRMATIONS

Notes

FOR TOMORROW

Today, I will.

Daily Planner

DATE ______________________ S M T W T F S

TOP 3 PRIORITIES

1.

2.

3.

MORNING

TIME   TO DO   TIME   TO DO

AFTERNOON

TIME   TO DO   TIME   TO DO

EVENING

TIME   TO DO   TIME   TO DO

TODAY'S AFFIRMATIONS   *Notes*   **FOR TOMORROW**

Today, I will.

Daily Planner

DATE ______________________ S M T W T F S

TOP 3 PRIORITIES

1.

2.

3.

MORNING

TIME	TO DO		TIME	TO DO

AFTERNOON

TIME	TO DO		TIME	TO DO

EVENING

TIME	TO DO		TIME	TO DO

TODAY'S AFFIRMATIONS *Notes* **FOR TOMORROW**

Today, I will.

Daily Planner

DATE ________________ S M T W T F S

TOP 3 PRIORITIES

| 1. | 2. | 3. |

MORNING

TIME | TO DO

TIME | TO DO

AFTERNOON

TIME | TO DO

TIME | TO DO

EVENING

TIME | TO DO

TIME | TO DO

TODAY'S AFFIRMATIONS

Notes

FOR TOMORROW

Today, I will.

Daily Planner

DATE ________________________   S M T W T F S

TOP 3 PRIORITIES

1.

2.

3.

MORNING

TIME   TO DO   TIME   TO DO

AFTERNOON

TIME   TO DO   TIME   TO DO

EVENING

TIME   TO DO   TIME   TO DO

TODAY'S AFFIRMATIONS   *Notes*   FOR TOMORROW

Today, I will.

Daily Planner

DATE ______________________ S M T W T F S

TOP 3 PRIORITIES

1. 2. 3.

MORNING

TIME   TO DO   TIME   TO DO

AFTERNOON

TIME   TO DO   TIME   TO DO

EVENING

TIME   TO DO   TIME   TO DO

TODAY'S AFFIRMATIONS   *Notes*   **FOR TOMORROW**

Today, I will.

Daily Planner

DATE _______________ S M T W T F S

TOP 3 PRIORITIES

1.

2.

3.

MORNING

TIME | TO DO

TIME | TO DO

AFTERNOON

TIME | TO DO

TIME | TO DO

EVENING

TIME | TO DO

TIME | TO DO

TODAY'S AFFIRMATIONS

Notes

FOR TOMORROW

Today, I will.

Daily Planner

DATE ______________________   S M T W T F S

TOP 3 PRIORITIES

1.

2.

3.

MORNING

TIME   TO DO   TIME   TO DO

AFTERNOON

TIME   TO DO   TIME   TO DO

EVENING

TIME   TO DO   TIME   TO DO

TODAY'S AFFIRMATIONS   *Notes*   FOR TOMORROW

Today, I will.

Daily Planner

DATE _______________________ S M T W T F S

TOP 3 PRIORITIES

1.

2.

3.

MORNING

TIME	TO DO		TIME	TO DO
○			○	
○			○	
○			○	

AFTERNOON

TIME	TO DO		TIME	TO DO
○			○	
○			○	
○			○	

EVENING

TIME	TO DO		TIME	TO DO
○			○	
○			○	
○			○	

TODAY'S AFFIRMATIONS   *Notes*   **FOR TOMORROW**

Today, I will.

Daily Planner

DATE ______________________   S   M   T   W   T   F   S

TOP 3 PRIORITIES

1. | 2. | 3.

MORNING

| TIME | TO DO | | TIME | TO DO |

AFTERNOON

| TIME | TO DO | | TIME | TO DO |

EVENING

| TIME | TO DO | | TIME | TO DO |

TODAY'S AFFIRMATIONS   *Notes*   FOR TOMORROW

Today, I will.

Daily Planner

DATE ______________________   S M T W T F S

TOP 3 PRIORITIES

| 1. | 2. | 3. |

MORNING

TIME	TO DO		TIME	TO DO
○ ____	__________		○ ____	__________
○ ____	__________		○ ____	__________
○ ____	__________		○ ____	__________

AFTERNOON

TIME	TO DO		TIME	TO DO
○ ____	__________		○ ____	__________
○ ____	__________		○ ____	__________
○ ____	__________		○ ____	__________

EVENING

TIME	TO DO		TIME	TO DO
○ ____	__________		○ ____	__________
○ ____	__________		○ ____	__________
○ ____	__________		○ ____	__________

TODAY'S AFFIRMATIONS   *Notes*   FOR TOMORROW

Today, I will.

Daily Planner

DATE ______________________ S M T W T F S

TOP 3 PRIORITIES

1.	2.	3.

MORNING

TIME	TO DO		TIME	TO DO
○			○	
○			○	
○			○	

AFTERNOON

TIME	TO DO		TIME	TO DO
○			○	
○			○	
○			○	

EVENING

TIME	TO DO		TIME	TO DO
○			○	
○			○	
○			○	

TODAY'S AFFIRMATIONS   *Notes*   FOR TOMORROW

Today, I will.

Daily Planner

DATE ___________________   S M T W T F S

TOP 3 PRIORITIES

1.

2.

3.

MORNING

TIME	TO DO	TIME	TO DO
○		○	
○		○	
○		○	

AFTERNOON

TIME	TO DO	TIME	TO DO
○		○	
○		○	
○		○	

EVENING

TIME	TO DO	TIME	TO DO
○		○	
○		○	
○		○	

TODAY'S AFFIRMATIONS   *Notes*   ## FOR TOMORROW

Today, I will.

Daily Planner

DATE _______________________ S M T W T F S

TOP 3 PRIORITIES

1.

2.

3.

MORNING

TIME   TO DO   TIME   TO DO

AFTERNOON

TIME   TO DO   TIME   TO DO

EVENING

TIME   TO DO   TIME   TO DO

TODAY'S AFFIRMATIONS   *Notes*   FOR TOMORROW

Today, I will.

www.ingramcontent.com/pod-product-compliance
Lightning Source LLC
LaVergne TN
LVHW080608200726
843509LV00007B/270